Best of Irish Poetry 2009

Scoth na hÉigse

BEST OF IRISH POETRY 2009
Scoth na hÉigse

Editor Paul Perry
Eagathóir Nuala Ní Chonchúir

SOUTHWORD *editions*

First published in 2008
by Southward Editions,
the Munster Literature Centre,
Frank O'Connor House, 84 Douglas Street,
Cork, Ireland.

www.munsterlit.ie
info@munsterlit.ie

ISBN: 978-1-90500-229-0

Contents

Introduction

It's been an eventful year in Irish poetry. And not only for the significant new books which have been published. It's a year which has seen Harry Clifton come in from the cold, as Fintan O'Toole called the publication of *Secular Eden*, his Paris Notebooks and his first book of poetry in thirteen years. In fact it's over thirty years since Harry published his first book and *Secular Eden* is a testament to his unflinching commitment to poetry and the continued intellectual poise and grace with which he writes. Justifiably, *Secular Eden* won *The Irish Times* Poetry Award at the Dun Laoghaire Poetry Now Festival this year. It's worth noting that *Secular Eden* is published in a beautiful edition by the American Wake Forest University Press, but not by an Irish publisher. Another poet whose book was published in America was Ciaran Berry. *The Sphere of Birds* was subsequently picked up by The Gallery Press. It's a beautiful book and a really stunning debut.

p28 •

Good poems appear not only between the covers of well made books, but also in the pages of Irish journals like *Poetry Ireland Review*, *The Shop* and *The Stinging Fly*. They appear in international journals such as *The Warwick Review*, which had a special Irish issue in the Spring of 2008, and Chicago's long-standing *Poetry*.

Newspapers also carry their fair share of poetry. Sinead Morrissey's beautiful dream-like poem 'Through the Square Window' appeared in *The Guardian*, but only after it won the National Poetry Competition in Britain. Other esteemed papers like the *TLS* and *The Irish Times* print poems regularly, but you can find fine poems in less celebrated broadsheets; the *Galway Advertiser* for example, where the sardonic and scathing lyrics of Kevin Higgins often find a home. Similarly, Alan Gillis's poem appears in what some might deem the unlikely *Ulster Tatler*.

p68-69

p49-50

p40-41

Dermot Bolger's poem 'Wedded' comes from a sequence of poems primarily in the voices of commuters undertaking everyday journeys across South Dublin County. An innovative commission, the poems appear as posters in such improbable places as Clondalkin Motor Tax Office.

Part of the pleasure of the editorial process was exactly this sense of surprise on discovering poems in places where you might not normally expect to find them. I could only choose forty poems which were published between July 2007 and July 2008 for this anthology. Given the go-ahead, I could easily have included more. But it was the unexpectedness of where the poems appeared that pleased me most.

Michael O'Loughlin, who has of recent assumed a Latvian persona in some of his work, the sardonic Mikelis Norgelis, broadcast his poem 'Parnell Street' on RTÉ Radio One's Sunday Miscellany. Whereas other poets have used the internet to disseminate their work. Justin Quinn's brilliant long poem of 108 stanzas 'Slavia' has its own website.

Poets find their inspiration from anywhere and their work, it seems, appears everywhere. That's my point: the best poetry these days can be found anywhere. It's encouraging to think about the range of sources where poetry can not only come from, but appear. Indeed in recent years Irish poets have been commissioned to write poems for such implausible media as beer mats and furniture catalogues. While some of these ventures may be whimsical, it does prove how pervasive poetry is within our culture. That being said, I was looking for work which would endure the year, outlive it, reward several re-readings and open up a space or 'a field of action', as Jorie Graham would have it.

I found the poems which began in one place and finished in an entirely unpredictable other place most appealing. Sara Berkley's 'Night Horses' and Leanne O'Sullivan's 'Lost' do this. The poem starts in wonder, as Philip Sydney put it, but does not always necessarily end in wisdom, but ends in

12

a new knowledge of something which was up to that point unknown. The kind of poem which seduced my editorial eye was a poem where a journey of discovery is made rather than any ready-made, preconceived argument.

Poets like Thomas McCarthy, Eamon Grennan, and Patrick Deeley, who are writing some of their best work to date, seem to do this. Their poems read as if the author is sometimes as surprised as the reader to where they have ended up. In many cases, to somewhere delightful and celebratory. In fact much of the work here has something of Auden's 'affirming flame' about it. I devoured Patrick Deeley's new book 'Bones of Creation' and marvelled at the consistent high quality of the work. It's refreshing too to see Thomas McCarthy, who has for a long time staked out an historical and political terrain, write one of the most erotic poems of the year in 'Well, Look At You.'

I regret not having been able to include more work here. One writer I know suggested editing this anthology was a sure way of losing friends and of making enemies. I hope not. I hope instead this anthology is one which you will come back to again and again, to remind you of poets you may not have read before or poets you have not read in some time.

A good year for poetry, so. And a sad year too. It was a year when Robert Graecen passed away. I'm happy to be able to include a poem of Robert's which was published in January, 2008 in the journal *Acumen*. 'One Evening' might even be the last poem he published in his lifetime.

This year was also a year when Paul Muldoon mused on an arts documentary about whether poets, when they reach a certain stage, should hang up their pens, so to speak, and avoid a process of self-parodying calcification. It was also a year when our most senior of poets spoke out on the proposed road to be built through the hill of Tara. Seamus Heaney talked of Tara as a 'mythological, spiritual

13

? Marianne ?

source - a source and a guarantee of something old in the country and something that gives the country its distinctive spirit.' Mr. Heaney's poetry and his public engagement continues to serve as a model to us all. After all, as Marriane Moore wrote in her poem 'Poetry', 'there are things that are important beyond all this fiddle.' Unlike the speaker in her poem, I did not read with contempt, but with awe, and I looked like her for the 'raw' and the 'genuine.'

Paul Perry

Paul Perry is the author of The Drowning of the Saints and The Orchid Keeper *(Dedalus Press, 2006). He is Programme Director of Aspects Literature Festival in Bangor, Co. Down and teaches at Kingston University, London.*

Réamhrá

Fáilte go dtí Scoth na hÉigse don bhliain 2009. Ní raibh de dhualgas ormsa ach deich bpíosa a roghnú don duanaire, agus ní mór an stró a bhí ansin. Tá sé suimiúil i gcónaí grúpa dánta a chur le chéile agus ainailís a dhéanamh ar na téamaí atá iontu. Sna dánta atá roghnaithe agam mar scoth na h-éigse don bhliain atá imithe tharainn, tá réimse leathain d'ábhair clúdaithe: nádúr, grá, cogadh, bás, dul in aois — 'sé sin le rá, mór ábhair na filíochta.

Tá idir mhór-fhilí agus fhilí nua bailithe sa chnuasach agus bhain mé an-phléisiúr as léamh na dánta uilig. Níl spás agam anseo díriú isteach ar gach dán, ach ba mhaith liom cúpla cheann a thaitin go mór liom a phiocadh amach.

I 'Machnamh ar Chogadh sa Liobáin', a bhí foilsithe i gComhar, deineann Cliodhna Cussen comparáid éifeachtach idir sheabhac agus lucht ionsaithe sa tír úd. Dán simplí, chumhachtach é seo; cuireann sé filíocht láidir George Gunn, ó Albain, i gcuimhne dom:

'Ó scioból
I ngort na mara
Airím an seabhac gorm
Ag marú na gcolúr
Ceann i ndiaidh a chéile.'

Sa dán 'Bábóg Rúiseach', Feasta, — atá cosúil le h-amhrán, áit a bhfuil an curfá 'Bain díom mo cheann / féach ionam,' — díríonn an fhile isteach go géar ar shaol mná atá ag éirí aosta. Tá an dán curtha le chéile go h-ealaíonta ag Ceaití Ní Bheildiúin, gach eilimint nascaithe i gceart aici. Tá an dán éadrom, meidhreach agus tromchúiseach ag an am chéanna:

'Bain díom mo cheann.
Féach istigh ionam,

15

bean óg ina seasamh
im' bholg, im' bhróga, im' lár.
Ardaigh amach asam í,
fág folamh mé im' phota,
síolta ag síolrú.'

Thaitin dán de chuid Louis de Paor, a bhí in Irish Pages, go mór liom: 'Cranndacht'. Tá na h-íomhánna gonta agus teann, agus tá saibhreas anamúil sa dán, cé go bhfuil cruth sách simplí air:

'Chuir sí crann caorthainn
sa ghairdín inniu
…
Fiúise, ar ndóigh,
a bhí uaimse,
cloigíní fola,
deora Dé.'

I measc na dánta eile a roghnaigh mé, tá ómós do Chaitlín Maude – an bhan-fhile is mó a thaitníonn liom féin – le Mícheál Ó Ruairc, 'Caitlín'; tá caoineadh ag Liam Ó Muirthile, 'Basáin Mhara', agus dán gonta le h-íomhánna iontacha ag Aifric Mac Aodha, 'Focal Cosanta'. Suigh siar agus bain sult astu.

Nuala Ní Chonchúir
Gaillimh, Lúnasa 2008

Night Horses

What I remember of it was the melancholy
innocence of those first rings on the river

and later the dark smudged fingers of rain
weaving the standing water into a garment with no seam.

The flood began to fill some ancient hollow,
then it overflowed that pool, found a new level

and began to rise: rain at the back of my throat,
behind my eyes, the silk of it in my mouth;

it ran through all the corridors of my house,
found the many corners, carried the pieces of my past,

a tide of fragments making collage at the high water mark;
it tugged at me as it went by, a lunar pull,

and as the chambers filled, the weight of rain
began to turn my world so slowly upside down,

the sky emptied its pockets, into the river
fell the milky moon and its veil of stars

and into the running stream I dropped my natural joy,
down it went, catching the light, a silver depth charge

until it met the river bed; on the surface
I stopped pitching, found my stillness,

and up from the submerged world
with its upside roofs and chimneys

rode the night horses with their unbridled stories,
and after them the green dawn and the songs of drowning.

Poetry Ireland Review

CIARAN BERRY

For the Birds

Something has pried open the body of this hare,
unpicked a seam from between the stilled hindlegs
to the middle of the slackened, gray belly.

Now the two sides of the wound part slowly,
like a mouth widening as it comes on the right word,
or that neat tear in the half-obscured lower thigh

at the center of the theater in Eakins's *The Gross Clinic*
where, as I remember it, the owl-eyed surgeon
seems so unmoved by the thick, scarlet globules

that glisten like cheap lipstick on his thumb
and the anguish a mother buries in her dress sleeve
as he explains precisely how he will poke

a scalpel into tendon, muscle, bone, to remove
the latest clot of gangrene from the left leg of her son
who might, if all goes well, last out the year.

Two assistants hold the patient down, while
a third and fourth, with their crude tools, keep open
the incision and stare deep into the mysteries

of the flesh, as eager for their time with the body
as the petrels, kittiwakes, black-headed gulls,
that tend the hare's remains up here in the near-

heaven of the dunes, all neck and beak and skirl
as they uncoil the intestines turn by turn,
divide liver from lung, pick out the heart,

squabble over the kidneys. Hauling away whatever
they can use, they rise through marram grass,
through shifts of sand, and disappear, leaving me here

to understand a little more what the dead mean
to the living, why every St. Stephen's Day
of that decade we lived on the outskirts of town

the same three freckled cousins, wearing straw hats
and masks, would bring to our front door
a single wren. One of them played a tin whistle,

his mud-scabbed fingers missing every third note,
another grinned as he held up their find in a jam jar,
while the third, his voice not yet broken, sang

a song about that king of birds "caught in the furze,"
that ball of roan and gray feathers punished because
its ancestor had once exposed the patron saint

of stone masons to those who pursued him
simply by singing from the wall the soon-to-be-martyr
had crouched behind. Like the saint, the bird

would suffer a harsh end—not stoned and left out
for the hooded crows, but stolen from its hiding place
deep in the undergrowth, fated to expire

behind that wall of glass, which must have seemed
invisible at first, when the boy's cupped hands
opened and the bird dropped down into its cage.
Half-starved as they stood there in old men's clothes,
those boys were also part of the cycle, and
would soon become their fathers so their fathers

could be earth, the oldest one driving a tractor back
and forth from the church, the one who sang
hanging dead rooks up in the fields to save the grain,

while the youngest boy, the one who held the bird,
inherited the title of village drunk and cleared
his mother's house of possessions to quench

a thirst that would land him face up in the ditch,
eyes glazed with a thin layer of ice, dead as the hare
struck down here in the dunes where, cold and prone,

the pistons of its legs proved no more than flesh
and bone, it lies empty as those blue tits Keats shot
to clear the air a few days after his brother

coughed up phlegm flecked with blood for the last time.
Keats, who was months away from his nightingale
and further still from Rome. Yet as he lowered the gun

to watch each ruffle of feathers fall to earth, he felt
sure the same blackness that had claimed poor Tom
was sprouting in his lungs and would blossom,

that his remains would mean no more than a dropped
apple to the worms the graveyard birds would yank out
of the earth and swallow whole, that he and each

of us would end up as coiled muscle in the wings
of house sparrows, a dull throb in the robin's fragile
heart, dissonance in the hoarse throat of a thrush.

The Sphere of Birds (Gallery Press)

PAT BORAN

Let's Die

'Let's die,' I say to my kids,
Lee aged five, Luca not yet three,
and under an August blanket of sun
we stretch out in the grass on a hill

to listen to the sea below us
drawing close, pulling back,
while the sheep on the hills all around
crunch their way down towards earth.

'Do you love the clouds, Dada?'
'Do you love the Pink Panther?'
and 'Will you stay with us for ever?'
to which I reply, without hesitation,
Yes, Yes and Yes,
knowing that as long as we lie here
everything is possible, that any of the paths
up ahead might lead us anywhere
but still, just in time, back home.

Like me, sometimes they act too much,
fill the available space and time
with fuss and noise and argument,
but up here, overlooking the landscape,
the seascape of their lives, on this hill
they like to play this game, to lie
together and together to die
which, in their children's language, means
less to expire or to cease
than to switch to Super Attention Mode,
to prepare for travel, to strap oneself
into the booster seat and wait and wait
for the gradual but inexorable lift
off and up and out into motion.

For my two boys, things are only
recently made flesh, made mortal—
our uprooted palm tree, two goldfish,
the bird a neighbour's cat brought down
last week—and they are almost holy
with this knowledge. 'Let's die now,
then let's go home for tea,' Lee says,
putting into words as best he can
the sea's helpless love affair with the land.

The Irish American Post

24

PADDY BUSHE

Black Dogs
For John P.

Hilarity, yes but also the only-half-smiling
Faces and tears of the counsellors
As we followed the wheelbarrowed body
Of the addiction centre's house dog
To the hedgerowed corner of the field.
Cara. Friend. Its name resonated
As the still shining black body
Was tipped easily into the grave.

I remember how I longed for a friend,
An anamchara, that first evening
As we filed back to therapy, each one
Of us digging deep in the clay
Of our own thoughts, each one
Aching to bury our own black dog.

Talbot Grove, 25 April 2007

To Ring in Silence, New and Selected Poems (Dedalus Press)

Moya Cannon

Still Life

Much though we love best
those rare intersections of time and space
where we are nothing but love's playthings,
caught, like two deer alerted in a clearing;
nothing but a sweet anonymity of flesh;
nothing but life's blessèd rhythm
loving itself through us —
two human bodies tuned to the whirring stars —

all this is almost nothing
without the small, quotidian gifts
which bridge separateness,
the small habitual caresses which hinder fears,
the grace of small services rendered —
two bowls of blueberries and yoghurt,
two cups of coffee,
two spoons,
laid out on a wooden table
in October sunlight.

PN Review

Ciaran Carson

Through

Irrevocable? Never irrevocable, you said,
picking me up wrong through the din of the coffee
machine.

We were in the Ulster Milk Bar I think they blew up back
in the seventies. We must have been barely acquainted.

Noise is what surrounds us, I'd said earlier, gesturing
to the wider world of disinformation, the dizzy

spells that come when someone you know might have been
in a bomb
as the toll has not yet been reckoned except by hearsay.

I'd have my ear glued to the radio, waiting for what
passed for the truth to come out, men picking through the
rubble.

Some of the victims would appear in wedding photographs
blinded by a light forever gone. Graveside by graveside

I shake hands with men I have not shaken hands with for
years,
trying to make out their faces through what they have
become.

The New Yorker

HARRY CLIFTON

Cloudberry

Mist and blanket bog, where the ice sheets vanished.
But it is here, according to the books,
Cloudberry is to be found –
In a single patch, on the north face of Dart mountain.
I can see you looking at me
As if to say 'What? In this weather?
Are rosehips, reddening haws and deadly nightshade
Not enough for you? Poisons, panaceas
Bursting from the hedges
Of half the country?'
Call it bakeapple, for all I care,
As the Canadians do. Alp and tundra,
Bog and blasted heath, are its chosen ground.
As for me, I'm through with life reduced
To the great indoors…
                              I want to go back
Just once, behind all that is Ireland,
To the age of free migrations
Where a man sets out, with only a Word in his head
And the needle of a shattered compass
Guiding him, through what is now no more than landscape,
With its huddle of frightened sheep
In driving westerlies, blown bog-cotton
Trembling like the beards of a million prophets
Leading their chosen peoples out of exile –
To eat of the tasteless fruit
Of universality, rooted
Like myself, in the invisible,
And belonging everywhere.

The Irish Times

Tony Curtis

In Praise of Grass

My father's three brothers
were Cistercian monks
at a monastery in the hills.
We used to spend weekends there:
my mother and father
cleansing their souls
while I played in the fields.

My father's three brothers prayed
harder than anyone I knew,
for me and the repose of the souls.
I shivered when they sang plain chant
praising God's blessings,
their voices softer than girls'.
I see them still,
lined up like soldiers
against the dark –
the light dying,
the air colder than the cross.

I liked the bells that rang
all through the night.
I liked that everyone was up
and out with the light.
But what I liked best
was to watch the monks work.
When they cut the hay
or went to gather in the cattle,
they were like little bits of autumn
moving through the fields –
brown leaves blown by the wind.
God knows I was never any good
at prayer, and yet,
when cloud passes along a hillside
or I look over an iron gate
into an empty field
I can still hear their voices
praising the grass, the snowdrop,
the leaf, the small miracle of rain.

Days Like These, Three Irish Poets (Brooding Heron Press)

CLIODHNA CUSSEN

Machnamh ar chogadh sa Liobáin
Iúil 2006

Ó scioból
I ngort na mara
Airím an seabhach gorm
Ag marú na gcolúr
Ceann i ndiaidh a chéile.

Ar shíofra gaoithe
Tagann na screadanna beaga
Chugam
Uaill an bháis
I mbrothall leisciúil samhraidh.

I ríocht an aeir
A fheidhmíonn an seabhac
Treallchogaí slíochta snasta.
Ná luaigh trócaire
Leis an tsúil ghlinniúil sin.

Comhar

Solitary
(Rusheen: Achill Island)

You may step off the old stone pier
onto the world at the ocean's edge, over boulders,
lichened rocks, erratics; the sea idling, long

arms of kelp sashaying in the swell;
you may be part of something, between-wheres
between-times, the distant islands shrouded,

the inland meadows dulled. In soft
off-the-Atlantic and persistent mists, you will stand
absorbed, flesh-heavy, anticipating spirit-shapes

and their whisperings as they pass, incautiously, by;
up on the mountain road the toiling
engine of a truck is an intrusion

yet a strong lien holds you to the invisible
and almost-visible, while you are relishing
the all-embracing ovoid bone-structuring

of the earth. Too soon this solitary existence
will have become so exquisite you will call
out urgently for companionship.

www.johnfdeane.com

PATRICK DEELEY

The Road

On our desolate walk
down this particular bog road,
we see five windmills
spinning whitely in the distance
        above the heathery hills.

But there's nothing we care
to say about them or
the shallow, cloud-haunted lake
away to the west of us,
and no surprises exist

any more – not the hundred
varieties of wildflower,
the thousand and one buttercups
blooming out of burnt
ground in the space the size

of our kitchen floor, not
the stone on a stone
haunched huge as any dinosaur,
not the old wrecked car
through whose bonnet

a furze bush is bursting.
For there are no endearments
we can spare, only
the dulled hurts, indifference
settling, nothing to do

but walk until the road
gives way, while all across
the blanket bog about us a swathe
of coarse grasses runs
with the will of the breeze.

Here the untenable path —
Twelve Bens jagging a far
horizon — turns us back towards
bungalow and seashore.
Despairing, at our leisure,

lost rancour, arguments
we've relinquished, the means
by which always at last
love led us to lose ourselves
only in rapture, before,

despairing. Then skylark,
so plain a bird, ascends —
sudden, signal enough
to make us exult as up and up
he goes, disappearing

in his song, but this kindling
something fit, spirited,
sensual. So we start, each
to the other separate, together
a mystery in our mending.

The Bones of Creation (Dedalus Press)

LOUIS DE PAOR

Cranndacht

Chuir sí crann caorthainn
sa ghairdín inniu

chuimil a préamhacha
sular neadaigh i bpoll

méara chomh slim
le duilliúr an chrainn

a roghnaigh sí
dem bhuíochas.

> Fiúise, ar ndóigh,
> a bhí uaimse,
> cloigíní fola,
> deora Dé.

Is fada léi, a deir sí,
go bhfásfaidh an crann
go dtí an fhuinneog i mbarr an tí
mar a gcodlaíonn sí,

smearadh cré
ar a lámha leonta cailín
is iníon rí Gréige ag siúl
na hallaí bána laistiar dá súil.

Tá rian fola
ar stoc an chrainn
ina diaidh
nach féidir
le máthair na báistí
a ghlanadh ná a leigheas.

Nuair a éiríonn an fhuil
i ngéaga an chaorthainn
dem bhuíochas, braithim
an chré ag análú go trom
sa seomra codlata in aice liom.

Go domhain san oíche
ionam féin, goileann Dia
racht fiúisí os íseal;
ní féidir a thocht a mhaolú.

Irish Pages

THEO DORGAN

Gaffer

She loomed up out of the near-dusk, quiet,
long-keeler, wood, gaff-ketch, maybe
fifty yards off. Coursing along, the hullwash
sibilant on her faded sides.
I roared at the crowd in temper,
where did he come from, there on the lee?
What kind of watch are ye keeping?
Everyone shrugged, I sounded unfair.
Ducked my head back inside,
could see nothing on the radar.

Hailed him, the solitary man on the wheel,
he turned to look at us,
tilted the brim of his cap, stared
off ahead again. Behind and inshore
the bullvoice of Roches Point.
The wind was fresh, I had a reef in
but he was carrying full sail, kerosene
running lights in his rigging, flare
of his port light a flame on the faded mainsail.
I took him for English, out of Dorset or Cornwall.

He flew no flag but everything there before us
spoke of an earned authority,
ease, the absence of doubt. For maybe an hour
he held station there beside us and
never again cast a glance in our direction.
As full dark came on we shook out the reef
and pulled ahead – light displacement, fin-keel,
the boat barely two years old. I wanted more
from this meeting than I could grasp, had sand
in my brain inside, some mind's infection.

We were bound for Kinsale but off the Sovereigns
something came over me, a sudden desire
to spend the night inside. We made in
for Oysterhaven, picked up a mooring
and settled to the tide. Over the south ridge
with its deep woods a sky of stars stood up.
I stood there smoking while down below
there was laughter, a burr of voices a rattle of pans.
Somebody's mobile rang, strident and wrong.

"Where do you think he is now?" Geoff, coming up.
We turned to the scribble of surf
in the harbour mouth, half-expecting that blunt sail
to blank the cottage lights. He must be staying out,
I said, making on for the west. The last red overhead faded,
a land breeze came up, smelling of leafmould.
Geoff rapped the coachroof with a knuckle, looked out
and away, said, "Forecast is good, he'll be okay."
 I don't suppose, I said, the weather bothers him.

Days Like These, Three Irish Poets (Brooding Heron Press)

LEONTIA FLYNN

Leaving Belfast
for John Duncan

The planes fly so low over the houses in the east
their undercarriages seem like the stomachs of giant birds;
the skyline in town is the ragged, monitored heartbeat
of a difficult patient; the river holds its own,
and for every torn-up billboard and sick-eating pigeon
and execrable litter-blown street round Atlantic Avenue
there's some scrap of hope in the young, in the good looks
      of women,
in the leafiness of the smart zones, in the aerobatics of
starlings.

There are good times and bad times, yes, but now you are
burning your bridges, and you are leaving Belfast
to its own devices: it will rise or fall,
it will bury its past, it will paper over the cracks
with car parks and luxury flats, it will make itself new—or
      perhaps
become the place it seemed before you lived here.

Poetry Daily

ALAN GILLIS

The Blue-Ringed Octopus Found On
South-Australian Shores

It may bring music to the living
room and light,
but the cable lies calm across the floor
like slack rope,
like an eel adoze in waters barely living,
if eels ever doze,

or like a tentacle dangled from a dying
conch shell, having turned
the colour of the conch shell at low tide:
the octopus
hidden like a lung. And he is dying,
who trod there,

toeing the strand's surf and suds and kicking
over speckled pebbles,
over the conch shell that lit to livid yellow
and sudden blue
rings that leapt and bit and left him kicking
his bucket in the sand.

And your skin was pale, but brightly,
like the living
room lit by that cable abuzz with the venom
of its voltage,
and your stark neck was tethered nightly
by the rope

of my self-regard, as I lay back to sing
Robbie's Angels
until your tongue unlipped its electric
and I crackled
in your eyes' smoky yellow, ice blue rings
in the dark.

The Ulster Tatler

One Evening

One evening in the dying light
As I wait for the old guy
She will come to my pillow
Though dead for years.
I'll see her young face
And listen, listen:
'Remember Ardnagashel
Our ardour that night
In the big house of echoes,
The ceaseless croon of the Bay?'
I'll cough and mumble:
'How could I forget you
Sweet lady of the manor
Our cup brimming over
As if for ever?'
Sleep now', she will say
And take my knotted hand.
I'll sleep and dream and sleep
The sea's croon in my ears
As I float away to Ultima Thule.

Acumen

EAMON GRENNAN

What Matter

Does it matter, moon at full, that moonshine
comes streaming through the bedroom window –
a shadow of mercury, luminous
in the early hours so the cats are wide-eyed
with anticipation, fretful at every whisper,
and we lie awake, counterpaned with light,
our thoughts free range, not to be tethered?

And does it matter that light, late afternoon,
makes every willow leaf, every mallard feather,
each bristling filament in the doe's freckled ear
show itself for what it is – a strand of gold
to airy thinness beat, a sort of spirit-tip to tug
us out of the big picture, put us in touch
with the far edge of things where the heart

has been in hiding, harking after what's taken
root there, distinct as dark-night starlight
but nameless, simply a sparking of inscrutable
integrity, a way of standing to attention
for a second, tantalizing the eyes out of your head
with hope, till the opening closes over
and your eyes and all they fall on

are only blunt, colourless stone? Day after day
does it matter that the heart of the matter
in the heart's heavy, loving tussle
with what matters – to eye, ear, finger-ends,
to all the tidal turbulence of the senses –
may rest in, may indeed, come down to, this
momentary unfolding to blind spots, blankness?

Out of Breath (Gallery Press)

VONA GROARKE

Marriage

How did the peacock feather come to be
found out in the yard, trampled, half-broken,
its wild eye tamed with dirt?

The last I saw, it was in the pewter jug
on the mantelpiece, so full of itself,
the whole room bent into its good grace.

You carried it so tenderly
across your open palms
as if it were a missive or a veil.

Lay it down there on the newspaper;
let it settle, unearth itself.
Then, we will get to work.

TLS

JAMES HARPUR

Kevin and the Blackbird

I never looked, but felt the spiky feet
Prickling my outstretched hand. I braced my bones,
My heart glowed from the settling feathered heat

And later from the laying of the eggs
Heavy, as smooth and round as river-rolled stones,
Warm as the sun that eased my back and legs.

When I heard the cheepings, felt the rising nest
Of wings, the sudden space, the cool air flow
Across my fingers, I did not know the test

Had just begun – I could not bend my arms
But stood there stiff, as helpless as a scarecrow,
Another prayer hatching in my palms –

Love pinned me fast, and I could not resist:
Her ghostly nails were driven through each wrist.

The Dark Age (Anvil Press)

SEAMUS HEANEY

Ref. p13-14

Lost Sight Of

i.

Who is this coming to the ashpit
Walking tall, as in a procession,
Holding in front of her a slender pan

Withdrawn just now from underneath
The firbox, weighty, full to the brim
With whitish dust and flakes still sparking hot

That the wind blows up into her apron bib,
Into her mouth and eyes while she proceeds
Unwavering, the container at arm's length

Ad horizontal in her tight two-handed grip,
Proceeds until we have lost sight of her
Where the worn path turns behind the henhouse.

ii.

Who is this, not much higher than the cattle,
Working his way among them across the pen,
An ashplant in his right hand

Lifted and pointing at me, a stick of keel
In his left, calling to where I'm perched
On the top bar of a rickety pen gate,

Pointing and calling something I cannot hear
With all the lowing and roaring, lorries revving up
At the far end of the yard, different dealers

Shouting to one another, and now to him
So that his eyes have left mine and I know
The pain of loss before I know the term.

The Shop

KEVIN HIGGINS

Ourselves Again

In the park our ice-lollies
fall victim to the June bank holiday heat,
while in glass rooms numbers moving
through dark computers
declare the future
finished.

Tomorrow, we'll have our double glazing
taken out; the crack put back
in the ceiling and a draught
installed under every door.
I'll attach a For Sale sign
to the seat of my pants.

Gangs of the angry unemployed
will bear down on the G Hotel
chanting "Down with the Daiquiris
and Slippery Nipples! Give us back
our glasses of Harp!"

In pubs nationwide, the carpets of yesteryear
will be reinstated, and there'll be meetings
of Sinn Fein The Workers Party
going on permanently upstairs.

On our knees, we'll ask
for the unforgiveness of sins
and life not lasting.
We'll be ourselves again
and then some.

Galway Advertiser

NICK LAIRD

Conversation

You can't believe the kind of thing
my kind go on about, and I in turn can't
understand the way your lot continually

shout, and shout each other down, and eat as if
someone's about to lift their plate and smash it.
I'd point out what we talk about we talk about

because we speak in code of what we love.
Here. Where afternoon rain pools in the fields
and windows in the houses facing west turn gold.

A flatbed lorry pulls out of the lane.
The mysteries of planning permission.
How someone got pregnant or buried.

The local TV listings. Bankruptcies.
Failed businesses. Convictions. How someone
put the windows in up at the Parish Hall.

How someone else was nailed to a fence.
How they gutted a man like a suckling pig
and beat him to death with sewer rods.

On Purpose (Faber)

The Lifeboat

I have imagined an ideal death in Charlie Gaffney's
Pub in Louisburgh: he pulls me the pluperfect pint
As I, at the end of the bar next the charity boxes,
Expire on my stool, head in hand, without a murmur.

I have just helped him to solve his crossword puzzle
And we commune with ancestral photos in the alcove.
He doesn't notice that I am dead until closing time
And he sweeps around my feet.
                              But it is Charlie Gaffney
Who has died. Charlie, how do I buy a fishing licence?
Shall I let the dog out? Would the fire take another sod?
The pub might as well be empty forever now. I launch
The toy lifeboat at my elbow with an old penny.

The Irish Times

Focal Consata
do David Korowicz

Leagtaí blaoscanna each
Faoi chúinní halla an damhsa tráth,
Go mbainfí macalla as sála bróg,
Go mbeadh na fallaí ramhar le ceol.

Ba choscrach an radharc iad, a chuid:
Foir'n an ghuairneáin mhóir.
Ní liginn a ndoircheacht lem'ais,
Ach ghuínn go bhfanfá im' chomhair.

Poetry Ireland Review

Thomas McCarthy

Well, Look At You

i. Correspondents

We make love after a long journey
Through the Sunday newspapers.
Our bed shakes with the crackle of the news—
Observer, Tribune, Indo and Business Post.

How far apart we were
While gathering such news.
Our stories for each other went astray
Like colour supplements.

You've always been my favourite reading—
A columnist who covered all our love-life,
Mary Welch Hemingway of the heart.
See how copy-editing you makes me lyrical,

Changing all contents to listen to your report:
Not the knowledge but the colour,
Not the bare fact but the facts bare. And this:
Fade to advertisement, your voyager's kiss.

ii.   Your Ordinary Gesture

By the time I reach the kitchen full of the most ordinary
          longing;
Thinking how we might extract ourselves from this life,
How we might find a place together in an unfashionable
          county,
Like O ...y, for example, or maybe the southern part of C
          .... W—

Somewhere less complex than a busy city – where the new
          pups
And the three cats can wander freely. At this stage, if I
          could have
You and you only, I'd go on the roads. No question about
          it.
Come with me, girl. During the war I dreamt only of the
          two of us.
Thinking thus, I smelled your Dunns' Brothers coffee
          brewing
And I caught you, before you became self-conscious, unself-
Consciously polishing your black shoes, dressed formally
For work. Let me tell you how that was, how perfect you
          looked.

iii. Oranges

You broke the blender
With too much spinning:
It sits on the draining-board
In shreds of afterthoughts

About doing dangerous things
With you: I saw the way
You force-fed it with
Oranges from Seville, you

As athletic and young
As any Crawford Art-school girl.
Where oranges sneezed for you
I make a simple, temporary bed,

A ledge where I drink the fresh juice
You made, that gulping treat;
Exhausted lamp in our ceiling,
Scattered rind of bedclothes.

iv. Your Silence

When the Italian novelist fell in love with your silence,
With the way you have of keeping things secret:
Well, that was the last straw. Unbearable love, that.
The way you un-gild the lily of yourself, the way
You hide a supreme gift like a child of countryfolk long ago
Running to hide some special gift in a countryside ditch:
That kind of reticence takes seven generations to speak –

So that when you turn to find an escape from praise,
When attention throws you, nearly, into a fit of rage,
I find you can be trapped more deeply in a husband's arms,
Soothed with my well-practised lack of praise, never
Lauded too lavishly. Ah, how you hate the smoothness
Of praise and all of charm's tiresome, inert complexities.

Clothed, unrivalled, secret, how Italian your gifts remain.

v. Watching the Olympics in a Maternity hospital

Exhausted by the effort, you turn your head
To me and I, misinterpreting as usual,
Presume that you are in an ecstasy of motherhood –
A kind of reverse for the mother's grief
In Synge's *Riders to the Sea*,
A female version of those victorious English runners
In *Chariots of Fire* or, indeed, Ronny Delaney
Falling to his golden knees in Melbourne, 1956.
But as I wipe your marathon runner's brow,
You maternal face that has trained for this
For years, through coaches and relationships,
Sponsorships, partnerships, pre-nuptial jumps –
You explain in a whisper 'It's oxygen.
It's a lack of oxygen. I need to sleep. Right now.'

A gentleman in a white coat taps my shoulder.
'Here!' says our Lord Killanin. 'Here's her gold.'

vi.   Shower

Beads of water fall from you
When you move between pine doors.

It is the hour after making love
And the house, with its kettle

Singing, its towel crumpled,
Allows in the orange juice of Sunday noon.

I think of the insufficient words
For this. Listen, words are hopeless right now,

Water clings to your beautiful self
The way we clung to our lives

Before we were strong enough to hold together
More than two metres apart. Showered woman,

The day glows like a young cigarette
Before us both. Your coffee is coming.

The Stinging Fly

Medbh McGuckian

A Novel About Patrick

Chapter the first

Second or third house on the left coming up,
Second floor, window twenty-one, I believe.
Window looking for a window, the window
At your back, sitting on the window-sill,
Watching the opposite pavement thick from strain.

As you read, try the word on, kingly plunderer,
To be found stolen in a century. You should stop
Using these minimum dreams as fuel,
I so enthusiastically underscore lines of yours,
I haven't been to the pawnshop in two months.

And right you are, never is, never was,
You just listen, listen — you hit the nail
On the head, you were as good as here, and burst
In you will, as if the presence of a faultless angel:
How two-in-one you are to me,

My soul is not that virgin. So he went on promising,
(Page torn) and this over and over, she was crying,
She was undressed by a man with your ring on his hand.
At the city limits she watched eighteen trains go by,
Her eyes cannot be paired up, sodden doorways of flame ...

Chapter the last

I am weary of cranial partitions and fabulously busy
Like giving birth for the twelfth time, and
As fate would have it, I have so far been unable
To take my place at the window:
You force yourself through solid crowds

On pilgrimages buying in closed shops, your pocket
Swelling with what was left over from the selling
Of a medal, pocket lined with smashed eggs
And sunflower seeds. Please don't think I have designs
On the days of the week, like verbs with holes in them.

The past is ripped off like a shutter in a storm,
A car cries out like a cuckoo, or coughs
Like an old ma opening desk drawers. Once
The sirens sound I hold on to the edge of my Remington,
From early in the morning, gun salvos broke

Into our house at any time of the evening.
I was that angel of modesty that heated your flat
With my Greek scent, I would scrupulously
Scrape my feet and clean my clothes with a brush
Moistened in disinfectant. I opened

The storm windows to air I had ceased breathing
Long ago, when I made that gesture of denial
Against your hands, with the waiter standing
Observing my mouth. New waves of the old feeling.
When the train came to a halt near the porcelain factory,

They said there was a storm on the lake, they said there
Was no storm. In a photograph I study with the eyes
Of two families, the city rises outside
The windows of the Hotel Octobre,
My book smiles at me anew, from the window.

The Warwick Review

Brian Moore's Belfast
for Gerald Dawe

The last trams were still running in those days.
People wore hats and gloves as long before;
raw fissures lingered where incendiaries
demolished Clifton St in April '41:
the big band era, dances and commotion,
but the war ended and rain swept once more
parks and playgrounds, chapel and horse trough
'to die in the far away mists over Belfast Lough'.

Do this, do that, road closed, no entry, stop!—
a world of signs and yet the real thing too:
even now I catch a whiff of brack and bap,
the soap and ciggies of the disparus.
Buns from Stewart's, gobstoppers from Graham's,
our crowd intent on our traditional games,
sectarian puzzlement, a swinging rope,
freezing winters, pristine bicycle frames;

school windows under the Cave Hill, childish faces,
uncles and aunties, pipes and lipstick traces,
epiphanies in sheds and woody places:
how can we not love the first life we knew?
'We can dream only what we know,' he said.
I know the whole length of the Antrim Road
and often dream of Salisbury Avenue;
mysterious Hazelwood, I still think of you.

On Riverside Drive and a California dream beach
such things revisited him, just out of reach,
just as he left them after Naples, Warsaw,
frozen for ever in the austere poet-war
where frequent silence keeps its own integrity
and smoky ghosts of the exhausted city
rustle with phantom life whose time is up.
They queue in Campbell's crowded coffee shop

or wait for a bus at Robb's. I can make out
a clutch of gantries, a white sepulcher
grimly vigilant on its tiny acre,
skirts and shirts mid-20th-century style
in dimly lit arcades, carpets of wet
grain at the quayside where a night boat
churns up the dark and a rapturous old girl
sings 'Now is the Hour' with her eternal smile.

Somewhere the Wave (Gallery Books)

PAULA MEEHAN

Archive

It is only after my father takes bad after Christmas
that we take the chance to get into his room.

It feels intrusive and yet it must be done
as delicately as we can tiptoe round it.

With the sorting comes the weary recognition
that after this small room the earth shall claim him.

I sit amongst his things in the wintry sunlight
dusting, washing, swabbing down and with a shock

I recognize my younger rounder hand there
in sheaves of notes in tattered folders.

I turn a page and soon am restored to Trinity classrooms:
W.B. Stanford and the Roots of Greek Drama,

Dionysias and Beatlemania – an aside,
The Peloponnesian War, Pericles, the Athenian Fleet,

The Cynics, The Stoics, The Tyrants,
The Republic and Hesiod's Works and Days.

It's all I have to hold my ancient confusions.
So much scattered in the squats and flats,

the vagaries of the road, the to's and fro's,
the wasted boys, those seasons down in hell.

There amongst my father's privacies
I forgive myself for the daughter I wasn't.

My Senior Freshman notes he deemed worth saving,
he who never spared a word of praise

or found a language of devotion except for horses.
Some comfort that this cache seems to say

that yes, he minded. Yes, I mattered to him.

PN Review

Black Loaves

We weren't given the game.
Somewhere, out there in the dark dust
Of childhood, we found it, discovered it bit by bit
And it led us on to the making of bread,
Baking black loaves, whenever the sun shone.

It was a summer of black clouds
But we were somewhere else,
Where nothing mattered much,
Below in the turf shed by the road,
Mould and water devouring us,
Sifting the turf mould into flour,
Mixing the black dough, sand buckets full of water,
Our postures changing, kneeling upright,
Sitting on our hunkers ...

Cheerful chatter, half listening to one another.
Dorry said she loved me and might marry me
Some other summer. Swallows flew in and out.
The dog stretched before us, her paws forward,
Eyes wide open, tail wagging,
Watching us mix the mould,
The black dough slipping through our hands.
Des lost concentration for a while
And drew a face in the turf mould with this finger.
Jimmy, who was working in the yard, shouted in at us;
What are you doing bedaubing in there?

Our hearts were full of black brilliance then.
Trays of turf loaves baking in the sun
Soon crumpled back to mould
But I still feast on the crumbs.

The Shop

SINEAD MORRISSEY

Through the Square Window

In my dream the dead have arrived
to wash the windows of my house.
There are no blinds to shut them out with.

The clouds above the Lough are stacked
like the clouds are stacked above Delft.
They have the glutted look of clouds over water.

The heads of the dead are huge. I wonder
if it's my son they're after, his
effortless breath, his ribbon of years -

but he sleeps on unregarded in his cot,
inured, it would seem, quite naturally
to the sluicing and battering and paring back of glass

that delivers this shining exterior...
One blue boy holds a rag in his teeth
between panes like a conjuror.

And then, as suddenly as they came, they go.
And there is a horizon
from which the clouds stare in,

the massed canopies of Hazelbank,
the severed tip of Strangford Peninsula,
and a density in the room I find it difficult to breathe in

until I wake, flat on my back with a cork
in my mouth. stopper-bottled, in fact,
like a herbalist's cure for dropsy.

The Guardian

PAUL MULDOON

See p. 13

When the Pie Was Opened

I

Every morning the water again runs clear
as it has for twenty years
of jabs
and stabs
where we've joined in single combat, my dear,

on a strand or at a ford.
Every evening I've fleshed my sword
in a scabbard.
The hedgehog bristling on your tabard.
Behind each of us is arrayed a horde

of heroes ready to vie
for a piece of the pie
with Hector, Ajax, Ferdia, Cú Chulainn,
and all the other squeaky-clean
champions who've once more forgotten to die.

II

Forgotten to die like the cancer cells
in their pell-mell
through an escutcheon-fesse.
The hot compress
on a pustule from which the puss wells

pus = claggy, infected liquid
puss = cat / facial expression
of dissatisfaction

as it welled for Job.
Every evening the impulse to disrobe
and take a little potsherd
to scrape the skin off whatever we've butchered.
Was there really a probe

into whether or not you would stand the test
of taking a hedgehog for your crest?
As if you might gather
yourself about a core
of high explosives packed into a vest.

III

A vest opened now like a dossier.
A badger with a white line running all the way
back from its snout.
Would that the world were indeed to be broken out
of its crust like a hedgehog baked in clay

by gypsies at the end of a lane.
Would that it were to hang from a crane.
The steam rising through a slash
where we've made a hash
of the whole thing. As for the bloodstain

on the cross-arm,
somebody told me vinegar works a charm.
Lifts off the whole kit
and caboodle like a pheasant at last making good
it escape from a peasant farm.

IV

A pheasant farm where we watched pheasant's ascent
translate into a dent
on our automobile. Wham.
I bet they could make out even on the jam-cam
steam rising from the vent

of a wound dressed with sphagnum moss.
Bosom boss.
The white line running all the way from the badger
to the gamekeeper-turned-poacher
who really couldn't give a toss

about having to share
her champion's portion of Brie or Camembert.
The minor obsession with glitz
from a major klutz
who's found herself enmeshed in a snare.

V

A snare in which we find ourselves enmeshed
as every evening our swords are fleshed
while Hector and Ajax
apply flax and white of eggs. The page is refreshed,

my dear, only as our servants bind
our wounds. A rind
closing over the Camembert or Brie
in some fancy hostelry
where we've wined and dined

in anticipation of putting on our gear
and stealing ourselves for the belly-spear.
The shit-storm
through a bloody stream
in which every morning the water again runs clear.

TLS

[handwritten annotations: steeling / [hardening ourselves in preparation for running the risk of being speared in the belly]]

Bábóg Rúiseach

Bain díom mo cheann
is rollfad ar an urlár:
    Rólaí pólaí, rólaí pólaí, stop —
    mó shúil ag stánadh aníos ort.
    Fág béalscaoilte ann mé.
    Líon an babhla,
    ól mo shláinte.

Bain díom mo cheann.
Féach istigh ioman,
    bean óg ina seasamh
    im' bholg, im' bhróga, im' lár.
    Ardaigh amach asam í,
    fág folamh mé im' phota,
    síolta ag síolrú.

Bain díom mo cheann,
féach ionam,
    maighdean seadaithe
    im' bholg, im' bhróga, im' lár.
    Ardaigh amach asam í,
    Fág ubh sa tsliogán.
    Suigh léi chun bricfeasta.

Bain díom mo cheann.
Féach ionam,
> gearrchaile scoile
> a mhoillíonn go sona sásta
> im' bholg, im' bhróga, im' lár.
> Ardaigh san aer í go sioscach
> is lig di spraoi le cupa a todhchaí.

Bain díom mo cheann.
Féach ionam.
> Seasann lapadán
> im' bhróga gan choiscéim.
> Ardaigh í is cuimil a com,
> siosama greanta ann,
> saol eile síolraithe inti.

Bain díom mo cheann.
Féach ionam.
> Éist le ceol is siolfarnach na bunóice
> im' bholg, im' bhróga, im' lár.
> Ardaigh id' bhaclainn í.
> Póg í. Soiprigh í
> thar nais i nead i nead an gháire.

Clúdaigh mé. Clúdaigh í.
Cóirigh orm mo chraiceann clasach.
Cóirigh orm mo chultacha uile.
Lig dom tostadh im chochall
ullamh don chlaochlú.

Feasta

Ionsaí Aoine an Chéasta

Aoine an Chéasta i mBaile na nGall
An t-iasc istigh is faoileáin ag seilg
Mar a dheineann mo mhac
Tástáil fhada ar an uisce:
Fliuchtar an chulaith uisce
Diaidh ar ndiaidh
Go dtumann sé go tobann
Is siúd leis an gcéad snámh.

Isteach i mo radharc
Tagann bobailíní dubha
Le mascanna is píobáin anála,
Glór láidir Bleá Cliathach
Ag gíoscán go trom
Ceol na bhfaoileán in iomaíocht leo
Is in ionad iascairí na háite
Tá speedboat lán le Corcaígh
Ag spalpadh Béarla ar an gcé;
Cuairteoirí lena ngiuirléidí costaiseacha.
An turasóireacht chultúrtha í seo?
Nó díreach léiriú ar rachmas na tíre?
Bréagáin nua as an SSIA.

Fós chím mo mhac
Ag imirt le feamainneach san uisce
Beag beann ar mo mheon.
Tá caisleáin le tógaint
Is uisce le treorú le dambaí gainí
Cuardach do phortáin
Is Gaolainn bhinn ina ghlór
Sé ardrí na trá é
A phaiste tochailte

Ullmhú déanta
Don samhradh atá le teacht.

Máthair an Fhiaigh/The Raven's Mother (Cló Iar-Chonnachta)

Nóiméad ar Maidin

Boladh na hiarnála,
ar maidin i d'árasán
ar Ché Hanover.
Tusa id' sheasamh
ansin ag an bhord
ag smúdáil
do léine ghlan don obair
is mé ag amharc ort.

Gluaiseann an t-iarann go mall
thar an éadach,
is dírítear gach roc ann.

Tá súil agam
go mbeidh rudaí eadrainn
chomh réidh sin, a stór.

Feasta

Nuala Ní Dhomhnaill

Na Murúcha agus an Litríocht

Cé go bhfuil léamh agus scríobh a dteanga féin acu
ó thángadar i dtír
is go raibh sí á foghlaim ag an aos óg
go dtí gur dúnadh scoil an oileáin síos
ag an Roinn um Oileáin Nuathriomaithe thiar ins na
      caogadaí
(baol ó mhaidhm nó sciorradh carraige an leathscéal)

níor thairríocíodar chúchu a bpeannaibh
is níor luíodar riamh leis an litríocht.
Níor chumadar is níor cheapadar
is níor chuir gothaí na n-údar orthu féin.
Ba scorn leo gnásmhaireacht an dúigh
is níor dheineadar a mbuilín
ar an áit aoibhinn aisteach úd as a dtángadar.

An Chistin Fhomhuireach,
An tOileán a bhí Faoi Dhraíocht,
Seanscéalta ón dTír-fó-Thoinn,
nó Maighdean Mhara ag Insint a Scóil Féin
cuid de theidil na leabhar nár scríobhadar.

Tá aithreachas orthu gur fhágadar é
agus caitheamh i ndiaidh an tseanshaoil
ar mhórán; mar sin féin ní bhíd ag cáiseamh
mar is maith a thuigeann siad gur fíor
nach bhfuil aon dul siar.
Is cé nach mbeidh a leithéidí arís ann,
beag ná mór,
ní scríobhann siad dréachta filíochta ná caibidilí leabhar
ag maíomh as.

Fágann siad na cúraimí sin
faoi na Blascaodaigh.

The Fifty Minute Mermaid (Gallery)

AILBHE NÍ GHEARBHUIGH

Gealach Ghorm

Lá sna naoi n-airde
is an ghealach ghorm sa spéir,
claochlaím

dúisím
gan drogall
roimh an gclog

téim
ar scuaird glanta
timpeall an tí

ní ólaim toit
ach uisce,
ocht ngloine

cuirim smideadh ar mo leicne
is bláthchumhrán
ar mo mhaotháin chluaise

leagaim béim
ar an ngealgháireachas
ar an ndea-bhéasachas
ar an ngansmálachas

Lá sna naoi n-airde,
tráim
is tránn mo dhán.

Poetry Ireland Review

Swell

Mid-March, on the daily a.m. drop-off
through a bunch of affluent side streets
between school and here

a refrigerated dairy produce truck
keeps catching almond and dogwood branches
so much that blossoms blizzard

the windscreen and moonroof
and I have to switch the wipers
to intermittent in its slipstream.

I scribble something along these lines
among the breakfast things and set it weeks to one side.
At first it doesn't seem worth the while,

to want simply to state that it was lovely,
that not every given is bleak or wrong
and some even are as gorgeous as they are elementary.

The kids come home on different buses
the same shade of forsythia.
We call my mother from the shore for Easter.

That poem with the truck and blossoms?
It gets bigger, hokier. I'm not bothered.
April's bright stretches, the mailman says, are swell.

Our local Y widens its opening hours a smidgen.
The clay courts opposite pock and shuffle.
I learn to swim.

Poetry Magazine

Menagerie

The ochre-coloured farmhouse at Gort Athaig
doesn't need much enhancing: but there's a story too.
At right angles to it, there's a wall: crude enough,
of breeze blocks half-whitewashed so the grey lines
show through. A group of visiting students
offered once to make a mural there, and did:
they painted tigers, lions, a giraffe,
and a bright troupe of circus horses. For years
the beasts guarded that turn that keeps away
tourist buses that can't fit around the corner.

In that wild-weathered place, overlooking
the finest landscape in the whole of Beara,
they lost their vividness in the course of time
until finally, preparing for the Stations,
they covered them with grey swathes of whitewash
(you know how marvelously it dries like snow).

The next April, Fosset's Circus – a thrilling mile
of trucks and caravans – came trundling out
of Castletownbere to set up in Killarney.
They missed the direct road to Eyeries,
and set off past Cahermore, over the Atlantic,
past Beirne's radio-mast and the coppermines
at Allihies. On they laboured, ten miles an hour,
gathering behind them an impatient line
of late-working tractors, vets, and dance-goers,

until they came to the wall at Claonach corner.
They couldn't get around; they couldn't turn back,
so painfully they uncoupled the wagons,
one by one, and overnight they penned
the animals in the sloping corner field.

Next morning, 6am, the owner of
the ochre house was driving back late
from a protracted wedding celebration,
and turning round the last bend for home,
saw them before her: returned from the wall,
escaped from their painted frame,
grazing in Gort Athaig above the sea.

TLS

Dennis O'Driscoll

Ever After

Whatever construction we put on
the mortification of the flesh by death,
whatever the happy-clappy euphemisms
we choose to shroud its devastation with,

there are few enough consoling glosses
to be put on a body scrapped in
tamped-down clay, trampled underfoot,
so reduced in means as to be human

infill, biodegrading fast, depreciation
setting in unless disposed of smartly.
We joke about it all, fall back
on bad puns, black humour,

wanting to sidestep negative
insinuations, stay true to the living
body, fend off morbidity, sublimate
our dread, stuff the unsettling

dead back into their crumbling boxes,
keep the snuff of their rancid dust from
getting up our noses, install granite
headstones to pin them firmly down.

The Guardian

MICHAEL O'LOUGHLIN

Parnell Street

'Death will come and will have your eyes.'
- Cesare Pavese

This is my first address: this is where
my mouth first opened. After half a century
I'm here again, as if the Rotunda midwife
Had never cut the cord.

Fair shades, my first loves
stand at the Finglas bus stops
Or shelter in the doorways of extinct pubs.
Here is the basement where young poets
Cuffed each other with sheathed claws,
The attics where we rehearsed our lives
As Songs by Leonard Cohen.

In the surprisingly beautiful Fifties flats
Behind the Georgian facades
I returned to film children
who saw religious statues move
the old gods' last performance.
Now the gods have gone
But those childrens' children
Still play on the streets,
Fearless and insolent as ever.

The world has followed me back here
Like multicoloured gum on my shoe:
Now I hear again every language I ever heard.
Drink beer I crossed a continent to taste.
The old Shakespeare Pub is a Korean restaurant
But nothing has changed. Men and women
Still face each other at tables, trying
To rewrite the night to a different ending.

In dreams I often returned here, looking
For my life, which was hiding
In an alley like a wounded animal.

Now I am afraid that
This is where death will find me,
Wearing your eyes.

Sunday Miscellany

Basáin Mhara
do John Keogh

Seolaimid an cuan amach
ag leanúint samhlacha éisc
ag sondáil ar scáileán,
ach ag brath ar do ghrinneas
caol ar an domhain
is tú ar an stiúir anois, atáim.

Bhí góstaí riamh ag éamh
os cionn an chuain;
na faoileáin gan anam
ar lánboilg ag guairdeall
thart ar an tigh solais,
scréachairí ina dtost go fóill.

Tá caoineadh cine crochta
ar aer na mara, an uaill ghoirt
a scuab sruth na muintire
san Atlantach, is sinne
leis an suaill béal amach
ag dul ag iascach basán mara.

Glanaimid linn go dtí an cuaisín,
áit ar mharaís breac go minic
cheana; faill ard ag titim le talamh
isteach ón gceann tíre, na slata
feistithe, inneall múchta, ag imeacht
le sruth, réidh don chéad chaitheamh.

Leis an díthrá ar an éadomhain,
is mó an seans iad a fháil;
crochann na línte ar bharr uisce,
is na clocha grinnill ag caitheamh
a scáil aníos agus sinn ag druidim
le talamh, is na duáin gan aon bhasán.

Maolaíonn ár seanchas ár dtnúthán,
is músclaíonn do spéis i ngach gné
bheo den iascach mo dhúil féin
gan ainéistéis sa bheatha, is an tonn
a bhraithim fém bhonn ar thóin
an bháid ag luascadh le sruth reatha.

Cuirimid dínn gan oiread is breac
a mharú. Beirimid ar na doruithe
is le cúpla tarrac tá lán buicéid
maircréal againn ar bord; cé méid
bíoga sa soicind sara mbíonn an dé
deiridh múchta ina gcuid putóg?

Fágann tú an stiúir fúm ag filleadh,
is le sracfhéachaint amháin siar
tugaim fé ndeara do lámha
liachta i mbun aclaíochta scine
ag sciobadh na bputóg as an mbreac
mara, mar a glanadh mo dhlúth
féin chun siúil le bás mo dhlúthchara.

Cork Literary Review

MÍCHEÁL Ó RUAIRC

Caitlín

na fir óga díograiseacha
go léir
a thit i ngrá leat
i bhfad i bhfad siar
sna Seascaidí
ba thú ina súile
an spéirbhean ab áille snua
an réalt gan cháim
an ógbhean uasal mhaorga
an réabhlóidí
an t-agóidí
an t-amhránaí
an file
agus bhí a ngrá éagmaise
gan locht
geanmnaí
glan
gan chnuimh an éada
neadaithe ann

agus táid fós linn
cuid díobh
na fir dhíograiseacha seo
is cé go bhfuil an óige
tréigthe acu le fada
fós féin
tá seilbh acu
ar an aisling
a gineadh ina gcroíthe
an oíche úd
ar leag siad súil ort
don chéad uair
an oíche ar sháraigh
an ghealach
ar an ngrian
lena solas geal lonrach
lena háilleacht
lena mealladh
lena macántacht

Comhar

Leanne O'Sullivan

Lost

Having watched the flashing shoals all day
he went out into the late evening with the men.
The mackerel and nets and the distant houses
seemed to be made from silver or a grey steel
under the moonless shroud of dark over the bay.
I watched the silhouette of my love's head
set like a heart in the boat, his back bent
as if he would heave them all out alone from the pier.

I felt it before I heard it, wiped it from my skin,
rubbed it on my lips, my eyes. It became as visible
as the lighthouse light icing through the shadows.
An hour before his boat went down I ran my hand
over his small bedside cupboard, followed the stream
of his mornings around the room. It was if the shell
of his breathing that billowed a shape in his pillow
suddenly waned, fell slack as a cheek in that nest.

When the morning rose I waited
behind the kitchen window, watching the sea lull quiet.
I thought of a blinding dawn, and the world underneath.
I thought of the fox-gloves waiting in the meadows.
I felt it before they told me, the cold, the tuneless shriek.
Up from noiseless landings the last few came,
bearing their knives and lure, their hands pickled,
moving like fish, rising slowly in the ebb-tide.

Poetry Ireland

JUSTIN QUINN

from *Slavia*
for Luán ó Braonáin

I.
I sit in Prague while at the airport planes
keep landing day and night and tourists crowd
through corridors of reinforced glass panes
towards immigration, dropped out of a cloud
then brought by taxis, switching through the lanes
past rows of towerblocks, the Europop too loud,
and is that the bandwidth or the money due
you wonder as the Old Town swings in view.

2.
It's January and the trees on Petřín hill
are black and brown, a tab of older dark
persisting from the centuries when still
the continent was wholly leaf and bark
and villagers had no choice but to kill
whatever creature bounded in an arc
out of the forest. They sent a speeding spear
into the hearts of boars and wolves and deer.

3.
Or something like that. All very organic
and probably they sang thanks to the beast
in some bizarre ur-Slavic or Germanic
before at last they chowed down at the feast.
Although the drum machine's a little manic
I have to say that overall I'm pleased
instead of ululations—here's a laugh, eh?—
they've got the Europop on in the café

94

4.

Or what about those places where the whales
sing you a duet while the styrofoam
they call your ten-grain ciabatta fails
to make its way down and you grip on chrome
and wonder if saving the world entails
consuming food whose taste is close to loam.
Big screens show kiwis in their habitat,
not on your plate. Oh for a deep-fried rat.

5.

The waiters joke and laugh among themselves.
They stand in such a way that, geometrically,
you cannot catch their eye. Unless some elves
appear and take some orders things might get tickly:
one man looks to explode, another delves
irritably back in his Apple. Wet trickly
perspiration gathers with each joke
and they decide to have another smoke.

6.

For Jesus' sake, has no-one told the waiters
there was a revolution nearby here,
right on this very street, demonstrators
with candles and songs, police in riot gear
and foreign TV crews with their translators?
A further street on Havel raised a cheer
when he stepped on the ledge. Before him there
a hundred thousand people in the square.

1.—6.
[7 - 59]   60.- 62. [63.- 68]   69.- 71.
(p.97)   (p.96)

72.—108]

69.
Do I remember this or did it come
from some crap novel or worse still a memoir—
one of the thousands promising to plumb
'the Irish soul' to choruses of 'Them were
the days my friend, we thought they'd dum di dum,'
by journos from the Indo who condemn war,
say their calling is to disaffect you all,
and fancy themselves as quite the intellectual?

70.
I catch a glimpse of Merrion Avenue
and think of all the roads that lead off it
through Pembroke's huge estate, the ground-rents due
on all the houses that I visited.
For decades this was what I came back to
after each trip. And then my parents split,
the house was sold and though the taxi's slowed
I have no reason to look down that road.

71.
For those few days in Dublin I kept alert
while walking through the crowds on Grafton St
and its environs: first, for bilge and dirt;
second, for buskers; third, for a way to beat
through all the people coming from a concert,
it seemed, slowed down from strides to shuffling feet;
fourth and lastly, to see could I distinguish
a spar of Czech in all that sea of English.

60.
'Another thing is all the fucking knives
that people pull when they get in a fight.
You can't just gawk at other people's wives
the way you could. As well, Turkish Delight,
Creme Eggs and Mars are shrinking and that deprives
us all of something. What a load of shite.
I'm not some cunt who'd rather dig the praties,
but things were better round here in the '80s.'

61.
I now have heard it all and watch the burbs
stream by. Monkstown. Stradbrook. Newtown Park.
And then Blackrock. The grass snipped to the kerbs,
the semi-ds and mansions, the warning bark
of guard dogs. Otherwise nothing disturbs
the money. Always such an easy mark
for satirists who had to get the work in,
as well as one-trick ponies like Paul Durcan.

62.
The sun cuts sharp and bright against the leaves
going lurid yellow, especially the cherry.
I grew up here to endless recitatives
droned by the priests who tried so hard to bury
their sex-drives in soutanes. Who now believes
those men suceeded? You had to be so very
circumspect and careful around them—
N.B., the lowered hand and lifted hem.

http://slavia.poem.googlepages.com/home

Snow

Even though it's dark when you wake
you know it has snowed. A chill silence
under the curtain. Cold glow on the wall.

And when you get up, on the sill you find
its perfect lid. You open the window
and touch. It takes and holds your hand.

Later you can run out the front door,
throw yourself on its mercy. But soon
you'll be back indoors, soaked and frozen.

Better to wrap up warm, spend the day reading.
Barbed wire of birdtrack. White branch
underlined in black. Cars asleep under ermine.

Soon the roads will open, their gutters run
with mush. Best to keep going, out to the edge
of town and on into snowquietened fields.

Here you can catch a missel thrush in the act
of burgling a hawthorn, watch it gobble rubies.
A bullfinch's rose coat, a blackbird's gold beak,

shine as if fresh-minted. Your own footprints
follow you wherever you go. And it's best
to keep going, through mauve and indigo shadow,

your own colours deepening, hardening into you.

Insert Your Life Story Here, University of Reading Creative Arts Anthology

Conversation

I put down the phone
and the years go by.
Twenty years later your voice
is unchanged, as if
as we paused to catch our breath
or press the receiver closer
our bodies lurched from us
and half our lives
fell through the conversation

or we go back and forth
and now as you speak again
I'm sitting on the floor
in an empty office in Merrion Square
clutching an antique phone.

Daily I abandon the typewriter
and the continuous paper
and leave the world on the table

to sneak a call through the crackle
as if we stood in ships in wind
and swayed: our two cities swaying
with small news. My copy's due
my roll of continuous paper
has rolled to the other side of the room
and now, mush later, years later
now that the paper's gone
and the line shut down
somehow the conversation continues

somehow we lie in swaying water
and never alter, somehow the line holds
and the years stretch, snap back
and we fall out, come to, send
our signals out, always
finished, unfinished, always
plugged in to a ghostly exchange.

The Warwick Review

DAVID WHEATLEY

The Recusant

At Burton Constable Hall
I have preserved in the old faith.
A chimneypot pigeon sits
like a hen on the rumble of prayer
from the priest hole below.
Let the fox in the long grass go home
hungry if only this egg might hatch.

Do not call this house empty.
The signeur has not departed
but vanished the better to linger
unnoticed. An attendant runs
a duster over the words
"deodand", "escheat" and "estray".

A sea-turtle shell, a sawfish snout:
the sea is a grave, and my cabinets
are the grave of a grave. My prize
whale rose to his fall; along
his spine's whispering gallery echoes
of his death roar carry and break.

About m'lady's silver powder
hangs a whiff of vinegared lead.
A frolicking Cupid smiles through
a marble scarf frayed to transparency
and asphyxiates slowly; Ariadne
is carried away on a panther's back.

A playbill reads In Preparation,
The burlesque of the ratcatcher's
daughter. A scurry of feet
on the backstairs announces if not
the daughter of the catcher, if not him
the rats. They have my applause.

Before they depart my last artist
And model will fill the one space left
On the library wall. One day you
Will feast on her breast and know beauty.
I shall call it "English School
(17th century, sitter unknown)"

TLS

Walls, Islands and Wells

for Mo Irwin

Can this be right? How last Sunday
to walk the Great Wall to a point
where it crumbled, merely a week
passes and this Sunday to be brought

round Omey Island, face the Atlantic and out
there a conference of swans, at our back
a hexagon fortress built for a writer.
Here a holy well with an alcove of supplications:

a dolphin's vertebra, a bag of miraculous medals,
smooth stones with girls' or women's names
scribbled upon them, a soother and a single sock,
everything one could wish for.

Then a ruined church of pink-granite
half-sunk in sand whose gable must glow
in the evening sun. But before the tidal
road back what stops me in my tracks

are sand-grains shifting with the speed
of an hourglass, revealing what sand
has been secreting,
the half-concealed Imperial yellow shell.

The Clifden Anthology

ENDA WYLEY

Gold Wallpaper

The night was ours—
young art students clambering up cathedral hills,
not afraid to force a window open, creak a door
inwards, brush cobwebs like a gasp of cold air
from our cheeks.

We were finding old houses
to make paintings in—you, a corner of shadows
to place your easel near, while I spent evenings
sketching the way starlight fell through cracked
glass and how the bone moon creaked.

Over ancient wooden floors,
ice-blue marble mantelpieces, the dusty mattresses
with the dent of those long gone still there,
the yellow light crept, a ghost across our canvases.
Old houses forgotten by all but us.

On and on we'd wander
up avenues swirling their yew tree spells,
scraping our knees and notebooks on the forbidden
chipped sills, our pencils and brushes scraping for life
while the rest of the city slept.

Until in one crumbling mansion,
your fingers touched mine and we stripped back
from the thick walls fat with damp, seventies swirls,
sixties floral patterns, the formal fifties lines—
and found gold.

Gold wallpaper lanterns and flowers trailing
delicate stems and light up to the shattered cherubs,
the intricate cornices, the tinkling, blackened chandeliers.
So beautiful we could not paint that night -
held hands and stared and stared.

Even now in the hush of our own home,
in the dark of our middle years, when your back
turns from mine in sleep, your mouth muttering dreams
I cannot know, I reach for you skin   your
and want to peel back time—

gold paper falling onto me from you.

The Warwick Review

BIOGRAPHICAL NOTES

SARA BERKELEY. Born in Dublin in 1967, her collections include *Facts About Water: New and Selected Poems* (New Island Books/Thistledown Press/Bloodaxe Books, 1994) and *Strawberry Thief* (Gallery Press, 2005). She has also published a volume of short stories, *The Swimmer in the Deep Blue Dream* (Raven Arts Press, 1991), and a novel, *Shadowing Hannah* (New Island Books, 1999).

CIARAN BERRY. Born in Dublin in 1971, he grew up in Carna, County Galway and Falcarragh, County Donegal. He now lives in New York City and teaches at NYU from which he received a Master of Fine Arts and where he was awarded a *New York Times* fellowship. His poems have been widely published in American and Irish journals and selected for Best New Poets 2006 and Best American Poetry 2008. *The Sphere of Birds*, his first collection, won the Crab Orchard Series Award of Southern Illinois University Press.

PAT BORAN. Born in Portlaoise in 1963, his poetry collections include *New and Selected Poems* (Salt Publishing, 2005/Dedalus 2008). His translations include Jean Orizet's *Man and His Masks: L'Homme Et Ses Masques* (Dedalus, 1998) and Alex Susanna's *Forgotten Music* (Dedalus, 2003). He is a former director of The Dublin Writers' Festival, editor of The Dedalus Press and presenter of the RTÉ poetry radio programme *The Enchanted Way*.

PADDY BUSHE. Born in Dublin in 1948, his poetry collections include *Poems With Amergin* (Beaver Row Press, 1989), *Teanga* (Coiscéim, 1990), *Counsellor* (Sceilg Press,

1991), *Digging Towards The Light* (Dedalus, 1994), *In Ainneoin na gCloch* (Coiscéim, 2001), *Hopkins on Skellig Michael* (Dedalus, 2001), *The Nitpicking of Cranes* (Dedalus, 2004) and *To Ring in Silence, New and Selected Poems* (Dedalus, 2008).

MOYA CANNON. Born in Dunfanaghy, County Donegal, her collections are *Oar*, for which she received The Brendan Behan Memorial Prize (Salmon Publishing, 1990), *The Parchment Boat* (Gallery Press, 1997), and *Carrying the Songs* (Carcanet Press, 2007). She is a former editor of *The Poetry Ireland Review* and is a member of Aosdána.

CIARAN CARSON. Born in Belfast in 1948, his poetry collections include *Belfast Confetti* (Gallery Books, 1989, subsequently Wake Forest Press/Bloodaxe Books) which won *The Irish Times*/Aer Lingus Award for Irish Poetry, the Ewart-Biggs Prize, the Irish Book Award and was shortlisted for the Whitbread Prize and *First Language* (Gallery Press/ Wake Forest Press, 1993) which won the T.S. Eliot Prize.

HARRY CLIFTON. Born in Dublin in 1952, he has lived in various parts of the world, most notably, in Africa where he worked as a teacher and in Thailand where he worked as an Aid administrator from 1980-8. He has published several collections of poetry, the most recent of which is *God in France: A Paris Sequence 1994-98* (Metre Editions, 2003).

TONY CURTIS. Born in Dublin in 1955, he has published six warmly received collections - most recently *The Well in the Rain* (Arc, 2006). *Days Like These*, featuring his work alongside poets Paula Meehan and Theo Dorgan, was published earlier this year by Brooding Heron Press in America. In 2003 he was awarded the Varuna House Exchange Fellowship to Australia. He has been awarded the Irish National Poetry Prize. He is a member of Aosdana.

CLIODHNA CUSSEN. Is mar ealaíontóir agus mar dhealbhadóir go háirithe is fearr aithne ag an bpobal mór uirthi. Tá saothar léi i mbailiúcháin phríobháideacha agus in ionaid eile. Tá trí leabhar déag de chineálacha éagsúla i gcló aici, orthusan *Gearóid Iarla* (BAC: Clodhanna Teo., 1978); *Inniu an Luan* (BAC: Coiscéim, 1987); *agus An Bhean Úd Thall* (BAC: Bord na Gaeilge, 1993).

JOHN F. DEANE. His collections of poetry include *Toccata and Fugue* (Carcanet Press, 2001) and *Manhandling the Deity* (Carcanet Press, 2003). *La Cité Stylizée*, a collection translated into French, was published in 1996. He is also the author of numerous translations and works of fiction. He founded *Poetry Ireland* and is the former editor of The Dedalus Press. A member of Aosdána, he was shortlisted for the 2003 T.S. Eliot Award.

PATRICK DEELEY. Born in Galway in 1953, his collections are *Intimate Strangers* (Dedalus, 1986), *Names for Love* (Dedalus, 1990), *Turane, The Hidden Village* (Dedalus, 1995) and *Decoding Samara* (Dedalus, 2000). He has also written stories for children, collected in *The Lost Orchard* (O'Brien Press, 2000). He lives in Dublin.

LOUIS DE PAOR. Born in Cork in 1961 and educated at Coláiste an Spioraid Naoimh, de Paor edited the acclaimed Irish language journal, *Innti*, founded in 1970 by Michael Davitt, Nuala Ní Dhomhnaill, Liam Ó Muirthile and Gabriel Rosenstock. *Corcach agus Dánta Eile / Cork & Other Poems* (Black Pepper Press) was his third collection of Irish poetry accompanied by his English translations.

THEO DORGAN. Born in Cork in 1953, his most recent publications are *Sailing For Home* (Penguin, 2004), *Songs Of Earth And Light* (Southword Editions, 2005) and *A Book Of Uncommon Prayer* (Penguin, 2007). His poetry collections include *What This Earth Has Cost Us* (Dedalus, 2008). He has edited numerous works and previously served as a director of *Poetry Ireland/Éigse Éireann*. He is a member of Aosdána.

LEONTIA FLYNN. Born in Belfast in 1974, her first collection is *These Days* (Jonathan Cape, 2004). She was awarded an Eric Gregory Award in 2001.

ALAN GILLIS. Born in Belfast in 1973, his poetry collections include *Somebody, Somewhere* (2004), which was short-listed for *The Irish Times* Poetry Now Award and received the Rupert and Eithne Strong Award for best first collection, and *Hawks and Doves* (2007), a Poetry Book Society Recommendation. He is the author of *Irish Poetry of the 1930s* (OUP, 2005) and co-editor of *Critical Ireland: New Essays on Literature and Culture* (Four Courts Press, 2001).

ROBERT GREACEN. Born in Derry in 1920, his poetry includes *Collected Poems* (Lagan Press, 1995); *Lunch at the Ivy* (Lagan Press, 2002); and *Selected & New Poems* (Salmon Publishing, 2006). *Robert Greacen: Collected Poems 1944-1944*, won the Irish Times Award for Literature in 1995. A member of Aosdána, he died in Dublin in April 2008.

EAMON GRENNAN. Born in Dublin in 1941, his most recent poetry collection, *The Quick of It*, was published by Gallery in 2005. Previous poetry volumes include *Still Life with Waterfall* (2001), for which he received the Lenore Marshall Award in 2003, and *Leopardi: Selected Poems* (1997). His poems have been awarded a number of Pushcart prizes and he received the PEN Award for Poetry in Translation.

VONA GROARKE. Born in Longford in 1964, Vona Groarke's most recent collection, *Juniper Street,* was published by Gallery in 2005. *Flight* (2002), also published by Gallery, won the Michael Hartnett Award in 2003. Other poetry prizes include the Hennessy Award, the Brendan Behan Memorial Prize, Strokestown International Poetry Award, and the Stand Magazine Poetry Prize.

JAMES HARPUR. Born in Britain of Irish parentage, Harpur now lives in Co. Cork. He has published four collections of poems with Anvil, London including *The Dark Age* (2007). Anvil also published his translations *Fortune's Prisoner: The poems of Boethius's Consolation of Philosophy.* He has also written on the Christian Mystics. Harpur is a former winner of the British National Poetry Competition and is currently poetry editor of *Southword.*

SEAMUS HEANEY. Born in County Derry, in 1939. Heaney has won the Nobel Prize for Literature. His latest collection is *District and Circle* (Faber 2006). RIP 30 Aug 2013

KEVIN HIGGINS. Born in London in 1967, he grew up in Galway City. His collections are *The Boy With No Face* (Salmon Poetry, 2005) and *Time Gentlemen, Please* (Salmon Poetry, 2008). He is the poetry critic of *The Galway Advertiser* and also regularly reviews for *Books In Canada: The Canadian Review of Books.* RIP 2023 Jan

NICK LAIRD. Born in Cookstown, County Tyrone, in 1975. His poetry collections are *To A Fault* (Faber and Faber, 2004)

and *On Purpose* (Faber and Faber, 2007). His novel is *Utterly Monkey* (Fourth Estate, 2005). He lives in London where he is married to the novelist Zadie Smith.

MICHAEL LONGLEY.   Born in Belfast in 1939, his collections of poetry include *Selected Poems* (Jonathan Cape, 1998), *The Weather in Japan* (Jonathan Cape, 2000), *Snow Water* (Jonathan Cape, 2004) and *Collected Poems* (Jonathan Cape, 2006). He is a Fellow of the Royal Society of Literature and a member of Aosdána.

AIFRIC MAC AODHA.   Born in Dublin in 1979, her poems have been published in several magazines, including *Poetry Ireland*, *Innti* and *Bliainiris*. She has won many prizes for her poetry and was recently awarded an Arts Council endowment. She is working on her first collection of poetry.

THOMAS MCCARTHY.   Born in Cappoquin, Co Waterford in 1954, his poetry collections include *Mr Dineen's Careful Parade, New & Selected Poems* (Anvil Press Poetry, 1999) and *Merchant Prince* (Anvil Press Poetry, 2005). He has also published fiction and a memoir. His awards include The Patrick Kavanagh Award (1977), The Alice Hunt Bartlett Prize (1981), The Annual Literary Award, American Irish Foundation (1984) and the O'Shaughnessy Poetry Award, Irish-American Cultural Institute (1991). He is a member of Aosdána, and lives in Cork.

MEDBH MCGUCKIAN.   Born in Belfast in 1950, her collections of poetry include *Selected Poems* (Gallery Press, 1997), *Drawing Ballerinas* (Gallery Press, 2001), *The Face of the Earth* (Gallery Press, 2002), *Had I a Thousand Lives* (Gallery Press, 2003), *The Book of the Angel* (Gallery Press,

2004) and *The Currach Requires No Harbours* (Gallery Press, 2006). Her awards include The Cheltenham Award, The Alice Hunt Bartlett Prize and the Bass Ireland Award for Literature in 1991. *Marconi's Cottage* was shortlisted for *The Irish Times*/Aer Lingus Irish Literature Prize for Poetry. She is a member of Aosdána.

DEREK MAHON. Born in Belfast in 1941, his poetry collections include *Collected Poems* (Gallery Press, 1999) and *Harbour Lights* (Gallery Press, 2005). He is a member of Aosdána and lives in Dublin. RIP

PAULA MEEHAN. Born in Dublin in 1955, her poetry collections include *Return and No Blame* (Beaver Row, 1984), *Reading the Sky* (Beaver Row, 1986), *The Man Who Was Marked by Winter* (Gallery Press, 1991), *Pillow Talk* (Gallery, 1994), *Mysteries of the Home: A Selection of Poems* (Bloodaxe Books, 1996) and *Dharmakaya* (Carcanet Press, 2000). She has also written plays for children and adults. Her awards include the Marten Toonder Prize and the Butler Award for Poetry. She is a member of Aosdána, and lives in Dublin.

NOEL MONAHAN. Born in Granard, County Longford, his collections are *Opposite Walls* (Salmon Poetry, 1991), *Snowfire* (Salmon Poetry, 1995), *Curse of the Birds* (Salmon Publishing, 2001) and *The Funeral Game* (Salmon Publishing, 2004). His awards include the SeaCat National Poetry Award (2001), the RTÉ P.J. O'Connor Award (2001), the ASTI Achievements Award (2002), The Allingham Poetry Award and The Kilkenny Prize for Poetry.

SINEAD MORRISSEY. Born in Portadown in 1972, her collections are *There Was Fire in Vancouver* (Carcanet Press, 1996), *Between Here and There* (Carcanet, 2002) and *The State*

of the Prisons (Carcanet, 2005). In 1990, she became the youngest recipient of The Patrick Kavanagh Award for Poetry, and has since received an Eric Gregory Award(1996); the Rupert and Eithne Strong Award (2002) and a Lannan Literary Fellowship (2007). She has twice been shortlisted for the T.S. Elliot Award, and has been Writer-in-Residence at Queen's University, Belfast

PAUL MULDOON. Born in County Armagh in 1951, his poetry collections include *New Selected Poems 1968-1994* (Faber, 1996), *Kerry Slides* (Gallery Press, 1996), *Hay* (Faber, 1998), *Moy Sand and Gravel* (Faber, 2002), winner of the Pulitzer Prize (2003), and *Horse Latitudes* (Faber, 2006).

CEAITÍ NÍ BHEILDIÚIN.

DAIRENA NÍ CHINNÉIDE. From the West Kerry Gaeltacht of Corca Dhuibhne, she has published two collections of poetry, *An Trodaí agus dánta eile / The Warrior and other poems* (Cló Iar-Chonnachta, 2006) and *Máthair an Fhiaigh/The Raven's Mother* (Cló Iar-Chonnachta, 2008). She writes in Irish and translates immediately to English. She has been published in *Feasta, Comhar, Go NUIGe Seo* and *An Sagart.*

CAITRÍONA NÍ CHLÉIRCHÍN.

NUALA NÍ DHOMHNAILL. Born in Lancashire in 1952 and brought up in the Dingle Gaeltacht and in Nenagh, County Tipperary, her collections include *Rogha Dánta/ Selected Poems* (Raven Arts Press, 1986), *Phaoroh's Daughter* (The Gallery Press, 1990), *Feis* (An Sagart, 1991), *The Astrakhan Cloak* (Gallery Press, 1992), *The Water Horse* (Gallery Press, 1999), *Cead Aighnis* (An Sagart, 2001·) and *The Fifty Minute*

Mermaid (Gallery Press, 2007). She is a member of Aosdána and lives in County Dublin.

AILBHE NÍ GHEARBHUIGH. ~GARVEY~

CONOR O'CALLAGHAN. Born in Newry in 1968, his poetry collections include *The History of Rain* and *Seatown* (1999). *The History of Rain* received the Patrick Kavanagh Award in 1993 and was shortlisted for the Forward Poetry Prize for Best First Collection in 1994. He has received two bursaries in literature from the Arts Council of Ireland and a Rooney Prize Special Award, and was Writer-in-Residence at University College Dublin in 1999-2000. He is a reviewer for the *Times Literary Supplement* and *Poetry Ireland Review.*

BERNARD O'DONOGHUE. Born in County Cork in 1945, his poetry collections include *The Weakness* (Chatto & Windus, 1992); *Gunpowder* (Chatto & Windus, 1995), for which he was awarded the Whitebread Prize; and *Outliving* (Chatto & Windus, 2003). Currently teaching Medieval English at Oxford University, he lives in the UK.

DENNIS O'DRISCOLL. Born in Thurles, County Tipperary, in 1954, he is a former editor of *Poetry Ireland Review,* and one of Ireland's most widely published and respected critics of poetry. His poetry collections include *Exemplary Damages* (Anvil Press Poetry, 2002); *New & Selected Poems* (Anvil Press, 2004), a Poetry Book Society Special Commendation; and *Reality Check* (Anvil Press, 2007). A member of Aosdána, he lives in County Kildare. ~RIP~

MICHAEL O'LOUGHLIN. Born in Dublin in 1958, his poetry collections are *Stalingrad: The Street Dictionary* (Raven

Press, 1980), *Atlantic Blues* (Raven Arts Press, 1982), *The Diary of a Silence* (Raven Arts Press, 1985) and *Another Nation, New & Selected Poems* (New Island Books, 1994/Arc Publications, 1996).

LIAM Ó MUIRTHILE. Born in Cork in 1950, he is a core member of the *Innti* group. His publications include *Dialann Bóthair* (Gallery Press, 1993), a selection of journalistic prose: *An Peann Coitianta (1991)* and *Tine Chnámh* (1984).

MICHEÁL Ó RUAIRC. Poet, short story writer and novelist in the Irish language. He has published four collections of poetry and six novels. He is currently working on a collection of short stories and a new poetry collection both of which are due out in 2007.

LEANNE O'SULLIVAN. From the Beara Peninsula in West Cork, she is currently completing an MA in English at UCC. Her first collection *Waiting for my Clothes* (2004) was published by Bloodaxe when she was just 21 years of age.

JUSTIN QUINN. Born in Dublin in 1968, his collections are *The O'o'a'a' Bird* (Carcanet Press, 1994), *Privacy* (Carcanet, 1999), *Fuselage* (Gallery Press, 2002) and *Waves and Trees* (Gallery Press, 2006). A founding editor of *Metre*, he is the current holder of the Heimbold Chair in Irish Studies, Villanova University, Pennsylvania .

MARK ROPER. Born in England in 1951, he moved to Ireland in 1980. His poetry collections include *The Hen Ark* (Peterloo, 1999), which won the 1992 Aldeburgh Prize for best first collection; *Catching The Light* (Peterloo, 1997); *The*

Home Fire (Abbey Press, 1998) and *Whereabouts* (Abbey Press/ Peterloo 2005). He is a former editor of *Poetry Ireland* and *Ink Bottle*, a selection of new writing from Kilkenny, and was awarded Kilkenny's Father Sean Swayne Art Bursary.

PETER SIRR. Born in Waterford in 1960, his collections of poetry are *Marginal Zones* (Gallery Press, 1984), *Talk, Talk* (Gallery Press, 1987), *Ways of Falling* (Gallery Press, 1991), *The Ledger of Fruitful Exchange* (Gallery Press, 1995), *Bring Everything* (Gallery Press, 2000), *Nonetheless* (Gallery Press, 2004) and *Selected Poems 1982-2004* (Gallery Press, 2004). In 1982 he won the Patrick Kavanagh Award and in 1983 the poetry prize at Listowel Writers' Week. He is a former director of the Irish Writers' Centre, and a former editor of *Poetry Ireland Review*. A member of Aosdána, he lives in Dublin.

DAVID WHEATLEY. Born in Dublin in 1970, he has published three collections with the Gallery Press, the most recent being *Mocker* (2006). Wheatley was awarded the Rooney prize for Irish literature in 1998 and the Friends Provident National Poetry Competition in 1994.

JOSEPH WOODS. His publications include *Sailing to Hokkaido* (The Worple Press, 2001), *Bearings* (The Worple Press, 2005), *Our Shared Japan, An anthology of contemporary Irish poetry* (Dedalus Press, 2007). He was awarded the Patrick Kavanagh Award 2000 for best-unpublished collection and is the Director of *Poetry Ireland*, a member of the Board of the Franco-Irish Festival and Imram festival of Irish language literature and also on the editorial Board of *New Writing, The International Journal for the Practice and Theory of Creative Writing*.

ENDA WYLEY. Born in Dublin, her books of poetry include *Eating Baby Jesus* (Dedalus, 1994), *Socrates in the Garden* (Dedalus, 1998) and, most recently, *Poems for Breakfast* (Dedalus, 2004).